Peculiar Plants of the World

Plants with Thorns, Spines, and Prickles

Beatrice Loukopoulos

PowerKiDS press
New York

Published in 2019 by The Rosen Publishing Group, Inc.
29 East 21st Street, New York, NY 10010

Editor: Elizabeth Krajnik
Book Design: Rachel Rising

Photo Credits: Cover (cactus) skynetphoto/Shutterstock.com; Cover (holly) Sue Kennedy/Corbis Documentary/Getty Images; Cover, pp. 1, 3, 4, 6, 7, 8, 10, 12, 14, 16, 17, 18, 19, 20, 21, 22, 23, 24 (background) Only background/Shutterstock.com; p. 5 Bildagentur Zoonar GmbH/Shutterstock.com; p. 6 (prickles) Kazu Inoue/Shutterstock.com; p. 6 (thorns) jurgal/Shutterstock.com; p. 7 margarita denisenko/Shutterstock.com; p. 8 Valentina Razumova/Shutterstock.com; p. 9 MM.Wildlifephotos/Shutterstock.com; p. 10 LanKS/Shutterstock.com; p. 11 Tom Vezo/Minden Pictures/Getty Images; p. 12 Victoria Tucholka/Shutterstock.com; p. 13 William Cushman/Shutterstock.com; p. 14 Dragan Milovanovic/Shutterstock.com; p. 15 Catalin Petolea/Shutterstock.com; p. 16 Anton Foltin/Shutterstock.com; p. 17 Rosalba Matta-Machado/Shutterstock.com; p. 18 Paul Vinten/Shutterstock.com; p. 19 Helissa Grundemann/Shutterstock.com; p. 20 Emilio100/Shutterstock.com; p. 21 D. Kucharski K. Kucharska/Shutterstock.com; p. 22 asifakbar/Shutterstock.com.

Names: Loukopoulos, Beatrice.
Title: Plants with thorns, spines, and prickles / Beatrice Loukopoulos.
Description: New York : PowerKids Press, 2019. | Series: Peculiar plants of the world | Includes glossary and index.
Identifiers: ISBN 9781538346044 (pbk.) | ISBN 9781538344910 (library bound) | ISBN 9781538346051 (6 pack)
Subjects: LCSH: Thorns–Juvenile literature. | Spines (Botany)–Juvenile literature. | Prickles–Juvenile literature. | Plant defenses–Juvenile literature.
Classification: LCC QK921.L68 2019 | DDC 581.4'7–dc23

Manufactured in the United States of America

CPSIA Compliance Information: Batch #CWPK19. For Further Information contact Rosen Publishing, New York, New York at 1-800-237-9932

Contents

Thorny, Spiny, and Prickly Plants

The plants living on Earth have adapted, or changed, over time to survive. Some of the more than 400,000 species, or kinds, of plants on Earth have adaptations called thorns, spines, and prickles. These parts help keep the plant safe from predators.

If you've ever been caught in **briars** during a walk in the woods, you know that prickly plants can hurt! However, prickly plants can be beautiful—like rose bushes and cacti. Even some trees are thorny. The plants in this book are peculiar, but they need their thorns, spines, and prickles to stay alive.

Plant Particulars

Thorns, spines, and prickles aren't the same thing, even though many people think they are.

The stinging nettle, a kind of plant, has trichomes. Trichomes are very small, hairlike growths that come from the plant's epidermis, or thin outer layer.

What's the Difference?

Many plants have thorns, spines, or prickles. Each of these parts is different. Thorns are sharp, pointed parts that are **modified** branches. They can grow to be several inches long. Most citrus trees, such as orange, lemon, and lime trees, have thorns.

Cacti don't have true leaves. Their spines are actually their leaves.

People often call the hard, sharp parts on rose bushes thorns. However, these pointy parts are actually prickles. Prickles are sharp, pointy growths that come from the stem's outer layers.

Spines are sharp parts that come from leaves or leaf parts instead of branches or stems. They help some plants, such as cacti, live in hot, dry places.

Supporting Life

Plants need certain things to live. Almost all plants need water, sunlight, the right kind of soil, and air. They take in a gas called carbon dioxide from the air. Using carbon dioxide, sunlight, and water, plants create their own food through a **process** called photosynthesis. This food gives plants the energy they need to grow and **reproduce**.

However, some plants don't get the chance to reproduce because animals eat them. Some plants have adapted different **defenses** against this. Some plants taste bad or can make people, **insects**, or animals sick. Other plants have thorns, spines, or prickles that hurt animals' bodies and mouths.

Plant Particulars

Plant cells have special parts called chloroplasts. Inside each chloroplast is a **chemical** called chlorophyll, which is needed for photosynthesis.

Plants can't move. Some use thorns, spines, and prickles to protect themselves. However, some animals, such as impalas, can still eat them.

Using Sharp Plants

Many people grow sharp plants in their gardens. Sharp plants can make good natural fences. Some people plant thorny bushes under windows to keep their homes safe from burglars. People may also grow sharp plants around another plant they don't want animals to eat. Long ago, people used hard, sharp thorns as tools, too. People in the Middle Ages made sewing needles from thorns.

However, some people grow sharp plants just for their beauty. Roses are some of the most popular plants because their flowers are so beautiful. People in dry places plant cacti to enjoy their colors, shapes, and beautiful flowers.

ROSES

Some animals, such as the cactus ferruginous pygmy owl, build their homes in saguaro cacti.

Dangerous Plants

Getting poked by prickly plants can be very painful. Some prickly plants are quite dangerous. Australia's gympie gympie tree has been known to kill pets and livestock with its tiny, hairlike needles. These needles deliver a strong toxin.

Mala mujer, which means "bad lady" or "evil lady" in Spanish, is the common name for *Cnidoscolus angustidens.* This plant's stinging needles can go through leather gloves. The plant's hairlike needles put a crystal into the skin that can cause a very painful **rash** called dermatitis. The rash lasts for many days, and the skin can look red, purple, or brown for weeks.

LEAF OF GYMPIE GYMPIE TREE

Plant Particulars

Other plants in the same group as *Cnidoscolus angustidens* are *Cnidoscolus stimulosus* and *Cnidoscolus texanus.* Both species also have stinging hairs.

Texas bull nettle is the common name for *Cnidoscolus texanus*. If its stem is broken, it gives off a milky sap. Some people may be **allergic** to the sap as well as the sting of its hairs.

Stinging Nettle

Stinging nettle, which is the common name for *Urtica dioica,* grows most often in Europe, North America, North Africa, and parts of Asia. Stinging nettle grows in shady spots along streams and rivers, in woodlands, and on **prairies**. When a person or animal brushes against the plant's trichomes, it releases chemicals that cause pain and an itchy, burning rash.

Stinging nettles have been used in **herbal** medicine for thousands of years. Today, people make a tea from stinging nettle leaves to treat allergies and some illnesses. A cream made from the plant is sometimes used to treat **joint** pain and skin problems.

Plant Particulars

Stinging nettles can grow to be 6.5 feet (2 meters) tall. They spread and form thick colonies using rhizomes, or thick stems that grow underground.

People sometimes cook and eat young stinging nettle leaves.

Spiny Cacti

Cacti grow in many places in the Americas, from British Columbia in Canada to the southern tips of Chile and Argentina. There are more than 2,000 species of cacti, which are some of the best-known spiny plants. Some cacti have long, hard spines, while others have fine spines that are almost like hairs.

Rhipsalis baccifera, or the mistletoe cactus, is the only member of the cactus family that grows naturally outside the Americas.

Plants can lose a lot of water through broad, flat leaves. Most cacti live in and are adapted to dry places. They need to conserve, or hold on to, as much water as possible. Their thin, needle-shaped leaves do the job nicely. The spines even give the cactus some much-needed shade from the hot sun.

Ceiba Speciosa

Ceiba speciosa, or the floss-silk tree, is very unusual. *Ceiba* means "giant tree" in a South American **indigenous** language and ***speciosa*** means "beautiful" or "showy" in Latin. The floss-silk tree has a bright green trunk that is covered in thick, cone-shaped prickles. The prickles store water the tree can use during dry times. Its fruit pods have black seeds surrounded by cotton-like fluff.

The floss-silk tree can grow to be about 50 feet (15.2 m) tall.

The floss-silk tree is native to Argentina, Paraguay, Uruguay, and southern Brazil, where it grows in **tropical** and subtropical forests. The floss-silk tree has beautiful flowers, and many people grow the tree in yards, gardens, and parks.

Gleditsia Triacanthos

Gleditsia triacanthos, or the common honey locust, wouldn't be a good tree to climb. It has lots of sharp thorns growing out of its branches. The honey locust's thorns start out soft and green but harden and turn red as the tree gets older. The thorns break easily once they turn gray later in the tree's life. The honey locust's seed pods can grow to be about 18 inches (45.7 cm) long and are food for many animals.

The honey locust is native to central and eastern North America and is grown in many gardens, city parks, and backyards. Its wood is used to make furniture and other things.

HONEY LOCUST SEED POD

These thorns are usually between 1 and 4 inches (2.5 and 10.2 cm) long.

Other Thorny, Spiny, and Prickly Plants

Many plants on Earth have thorns, spines, or prickles. *Mammillaria balsasoides*, which is commonly called fishhook cactus, is a species of cactus that has long, hooked, dark brown spines and large yellow flowers.

Some plants aren't sharp in the same sense as the other plants covered in this book. *Sansevieria* plants, or snake plants, are common houseplants that have hard or soft leaves that grow to a point. Holly plants also have points and spiny edges on their leaves.

Sharp plants play an important part in their surroundings. Without them, some animals wouldn't have food or homes.

SNAKE PLANT

Glossary

allergic: Having an allergy, or a condition in which a person is made sick by something that is harmless to most people.

briar: A wild plant with many sharp points on its branches.

chemical: Matter that can be mixed with other matter to cause changes.

defense: A feature of a living thing that helps keep it safe.

herbal: Made of or relating to herbs, or a plant or plant part used in medicine or in seasoning foods.

indigenous: Naturally found in a particular region.

insect: A small animal that has six legs and a body formed of three parts that may have wings.

joint: A point where two bones meet in the body.

modify: To make changes to something.

prairie: A large, mostly flat area of land in North America that has few trees and is covered in grasses.

process: A set of actions that produce something or that lead to a particular result.

rash: A breaking out of the skin with red spots from illness or an allergic reaction.

reproduce: To produce another living thing of the same kind.

tropical: Of, relating to, or occurring in the tropics.

Index

Websites

Due to the changing nature of Internet links, PowerKids Press has developed an online list of websites related to the subject of this book. This site is updated regularly. Please use this link to access the list: www.powerkidslinks.com/ppw/thorns